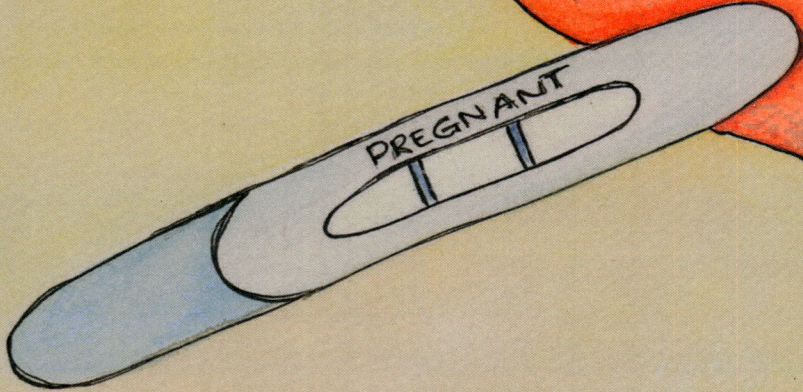

Miss Carried

First published in Australia by Petra Jankulovski 2025

Copyright © Petra Jankulovski 2025
All Rights Reserved

A catalogue record for this
book is available from the
National Library of Australia

ISBN: 978-1-7638588-0-0 (pbk)
ISBN: 978-1-7638588-1-7 (ebk)

Artwork and photography by Georgie Lyn © 2025

Typesetting and design by Publicious Book Publishing
Published in collaboration with Publicious Book Publishing
www.publicious.com.au

This book is dedicated to my one and only daughter. She is my daily reminder that hope can lead to happiness.

Wow, I'm growing a human.
I have superpowers!

Doctor, "Congratulations, your baby has a strong heartbeat."

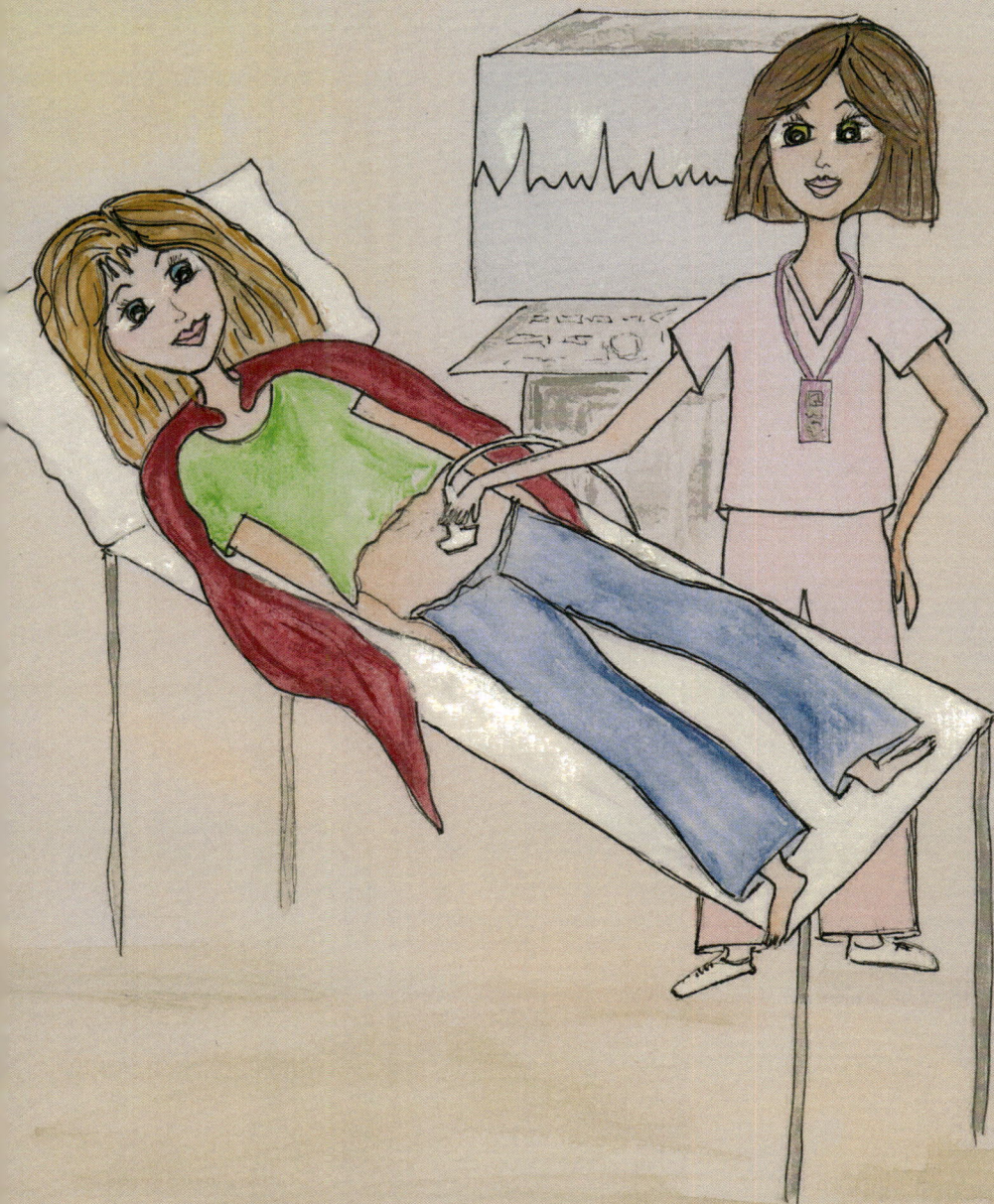

'NESTING.'

"Something is
not right!"

"Please let everything be ok."

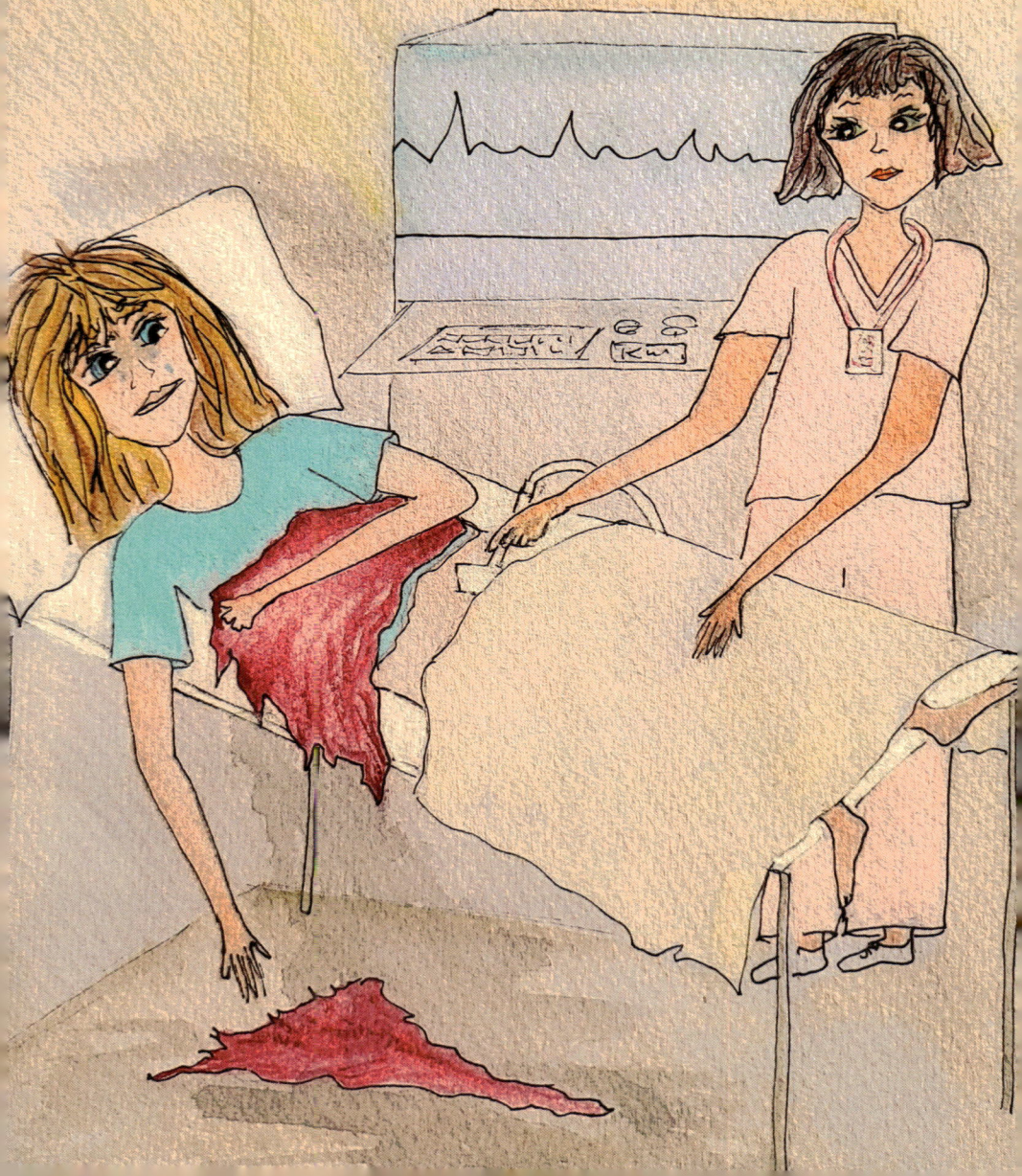

Doctor, "I am so sorry, there is no heartbeat. You will miscarry"

Receptionist, "That will be $$ for today."

"And just like that, my world has changed."

Later that night…

Early morning…

Doctor, "Everything went well.
It will be ok; you can try again."

'NUMB.'

'GRIEF.'

'GUILT – SELF BLAME.'

'HOPELESSNESS.'

'ANGER.'

"I'm ok, I've got this."

"I'm not ok."

'STUCK.'

Dad, "Baby girl, let me carry your pain,
so you can rest and heal."

'SEEKING HELP.'

'STRENGTH.'

'HOPE.'

'HAPPINESS'

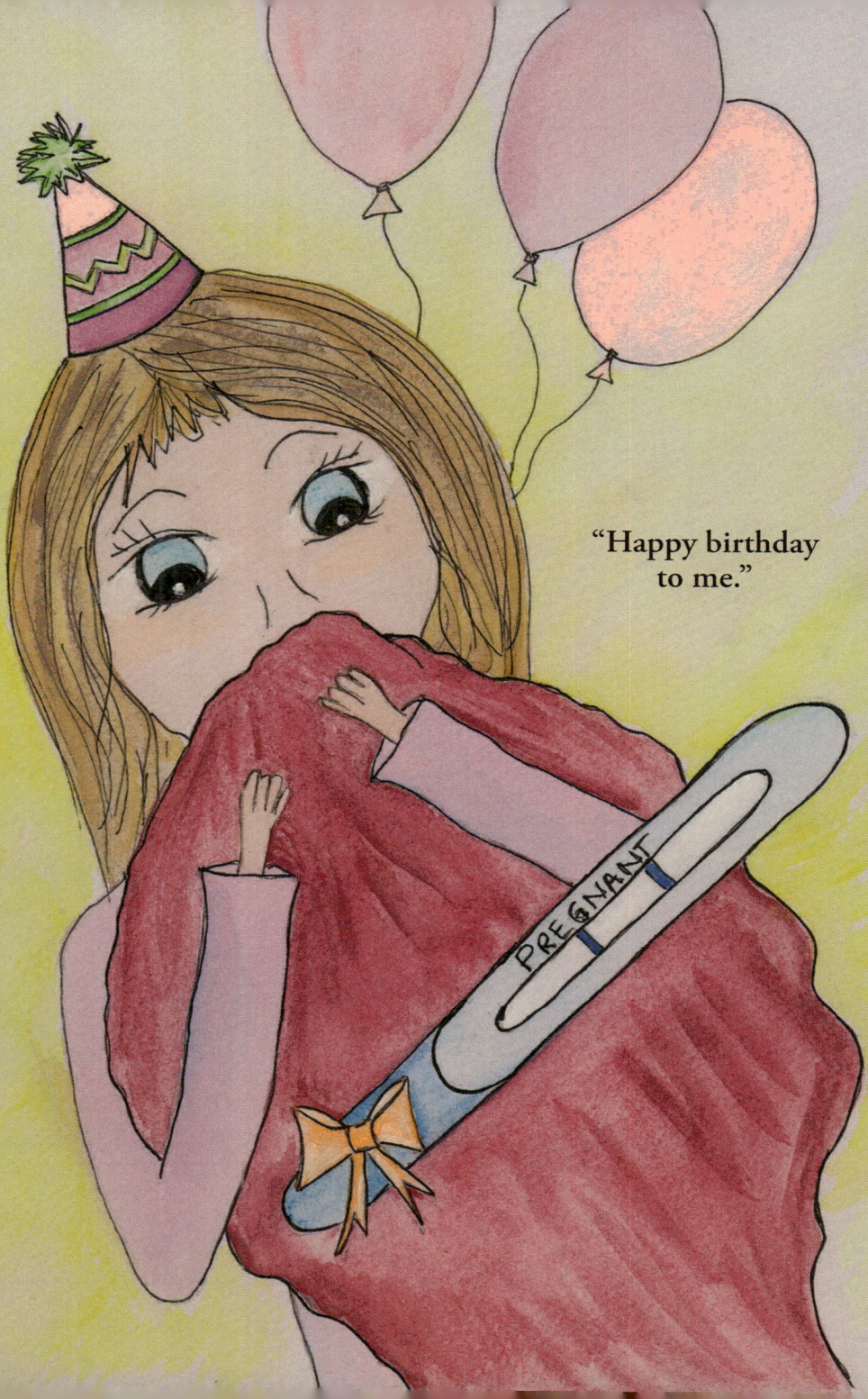

"Happy birthday to me."

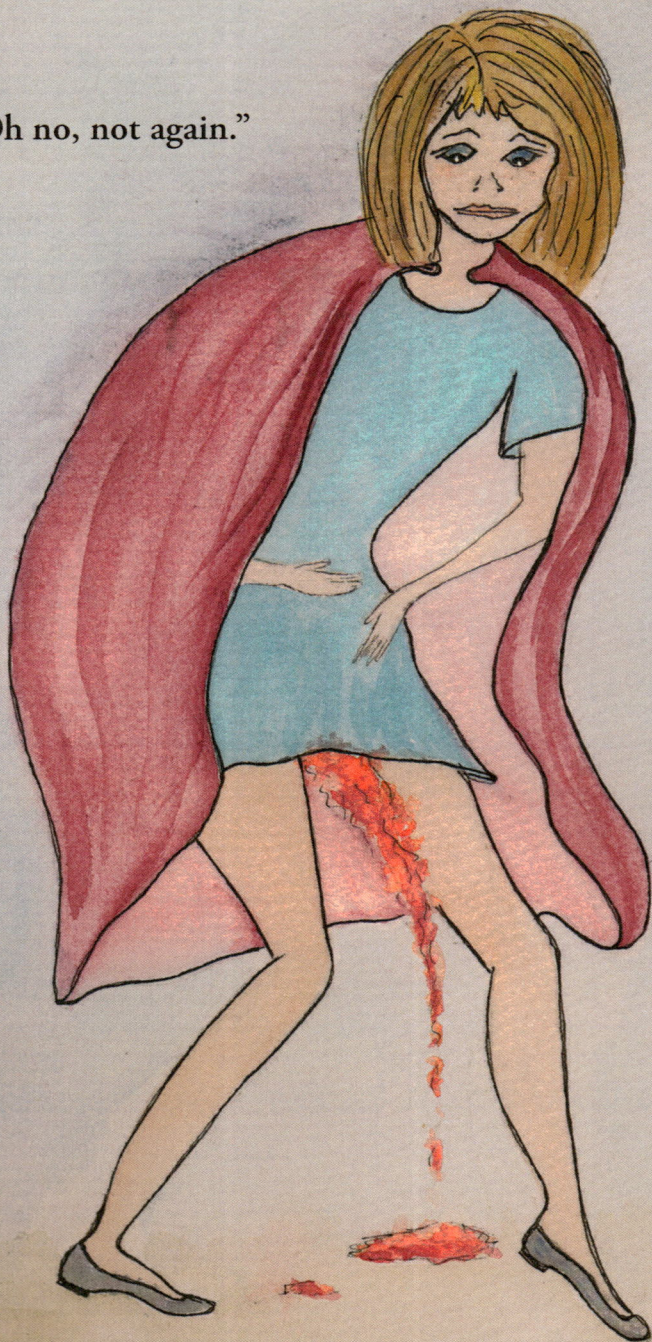

"Oh no, not again."

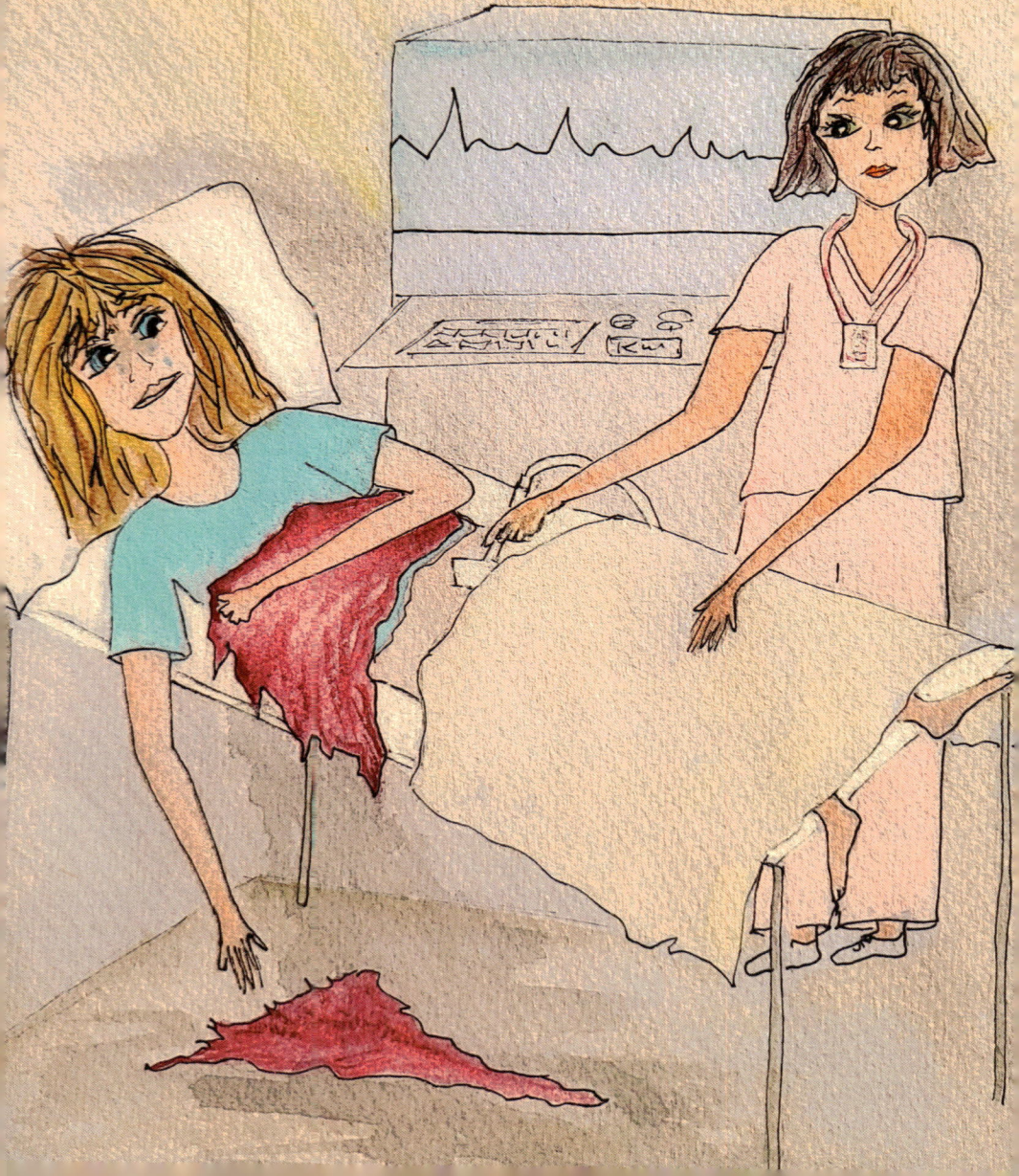

Doctor, "You have two babies. One did not survive, but the other has a strong heartbeat."

"I need to be strong and carry the sad me through this."

'PEACE.'

Petra is a single Mum, who lives by the seaside in Melbourne. She and her daughter have chosen to live a life with a focus on peace, harmony and kindness. When she's not creating pictures in her head, she is teaching care staff across Australia how to handle complaints using her humanitarian approach. Her mission is to provide hope, through illustrations, for women who are facing challenges.

Acknowledgement: To my illustrator, Georgie. Thank you for taking my vision and putting it on paper. Thank you for drawing from the heart and stepping into my shoes, without judgement. You have become my life long friend. This is only the beginning. So many more stories to be told.